WHAT'S IN A NAME?
UNAITWAJE?
A SWAHILI BOOK OF NAMES

Africa World Press, Inc.
P.O. Box 1892
Trenton, N. J. 08607

© copyright 1993
by Sharifa M. Zawawi
First Printing 1993

Series Conception: Ife Designs
Book Design: Jonathan Gullery

Illustrations
From *African Designs from Traditional Sources* by Geoffrey Williams

Library of Congress Cataloging-in-Publication Data

Zawawi, Sharifa.
What's in a name = Unaitwaje? : a Swahili book of names /
Sharifa M. Zawawi.
p.   cm.
Includes bibliographical references.
ISBN 0-86543-290-2 — ISBN 0-86543-291-0 (pbk.)
1. Names, Personal--Africa, East--Dictionaries. 2. Names,
Personal--Swahili--Dictionaries. I. Title. II. Title: Unaitwaje?
CS2375.A353Z39   1993
929.4 ' 08896392--dc20   93-14859
                                                              CIP

WHAT'S IN A NAME?
UNAITWAJE?
A SWAHILI BOOK OF NAMES

SHARIFA M. ZAWAWI

Africa World Press, Inc.

P.O. Box 1892
Trenton, New Jersey 08607

I would like to dedicate this book to all my students, past and present, of The City College of the City University of New York, Columbia University, and New York University and to their children.

ACKNOWLEDGEMENT

I would like to express my gratitude to many relatives and friends who have helped me compile these names. They are too many for me to list by name each and every one. I am very grateful for their suggestions, and I am lucky and honored to know them.

I would like, however, to single out two people, Dr. Joan Vincent of Barnard College, Columbia University and Dr. Miriam Drabkin, professor emerita of The City College of the City University of New York, for reading, reviewing and editing the manuscript. Without their valuable help, I could not have completed this book. The errors and omissions are my own responsibility. I would also like to thank my publisher Mr. Kassahun Checole, who urged me to write this book and for his effective persuasion and encouragement. His commitment and involvement in publishing and distributing books on Africa is commendable. And to my readers, past and present, thank you all.

TABLE OF CONTENTS

PART ONE:
WHAT'S IN A NAME?

PART ONE:
WHAT'S IN A NAME?[1]

INTRODUCTION

This Kiswahili name book is written at the request of its publisher, Africa World Press. Most books about African names have included in their discussions names used by Swahili speaking people but the present book is different.[2] It is mostly about the personal names used by the Waswahili people and tells of the meanings these names have.

Besides having a psychological role in establishing a person's identity, names convey, to those who know their origin and meaning, the social and cultural existence of the people who have created them. They also reveal the historical and political contacts of the Swahili speaking people throughout their long history and their interrelationships with one another within the complex Swahili culture. Above all, names depict how members of a community see and regard themselves.

Recently, the adoption of Swahili names by people from continents other than Africa has enriched a cultural movement by means of which minorities have chosen proudly to construct new-found common identities. Personal names represent only one aspect of their culture but an important one.

In this book the Waswahili are identified as those people who speak Kiswahili (of any dialect) as their first language and share in its culture. These comprise African people and people of African descent, of different tribal and ethnic identities, who have a common language and culture. In this book I have included names with which I am well acquainted, as well as some which relatives and friends have suggested to me, and some that I have come across in my reading of Swahili literature.

You will find listed African indigineous, Biblical and Islamic names all of which are in use in East Africa today. Many of them represent a lexicon that could be used by different people irrespective of their religion or ethnic group. Many of the religious or historical names suggest a common origin. They are most likely of common origin and derive from some common ancestor language. This language has been variously identified by scholars as Sumerian, Semitic, Akkadian, Aramaic, Syriac, Kananite, Phoenician (Finiiqii), Bantu, Azanian, Egyptian, Kemet (Q-m-t), Hamito-Semitic and Afro-Asiatic.

A good example of our common human identity is to be found in the Swahili name *mwanaadamu* (human being). This is a compound word made up of three parts. First comes the personal prefix *mu-* which becomes in Swahili *mw-* in front of a vowel. This prefix occurs in many African languages as well as in Semitic languages, including Aramaic, Arabic and Ethiopian languages such as Tigrinya and Amharic and, perhaps, Ge'ez (Ghiiz). The second component is *-ana* meaning person, an African word which is equivalent to the Arabic anaam (mankind). In Swahili this also appears in the words *mwana* (person), *mwanamke* (woman) and *mwanamme* (man). The third part *adam* means, in Islam and in Arabic, the first man. Its origin is said to be Phoenician. This may be equivalent to the Hebrew word for red earth or Persian for brownish. The Scots have their son of Adam in the name MacAdam or McAdam. As human beings we are different in many respects but we share many similarities as well.

This little book should be of use not only to the young people for whom, primarily, it is written, but also to adults who might be interested in learning about the personal names used in a particular region in Africa and their significance.

TERMINOLOGY

In the English language the word name labels identity, an expression by which a person, a thing, or a place is mentioned or identified. The Arabic equivalent to this word is the root nam meaning essence, relate or inform about one. The verb *namma* in Arabic means to trace one's origin or roots, belongingness and growth.[3]

The Arab speaker has also another word, *ism*, for name, which originates in the root *s-m*. In its second grammatical form of samma it denotes a level of relationship, raising one to a level.

A Swahili speaker uses another expression, *jina*, for name. This is derived from -*'iin* meaning to show or to identify. Thus all three roots :-*nam*,-*s-m* and -*'iin* which represent the English name, Arabic *ism*, and Swahili *jina* respectively signify an identity. Through your name people see who you are. The Waswahili people have a superstition that a person may also be harmed through his or her name.[4]

WHAT IS YOUR NAME?
Jina Lako Nani?

If you were born in East Africa, into Swahili society, your name, *jina lako*, was your initiation into your society. Most likely it preceded you. It was in use before you were born and it was waiting for you before you were born. Someone chose it; you did not select it for yourself. Your parents or grandparents, your elder brother or sister chose it, on your behalf, with love and affection. Or it might have been suggested by a more distant relative or a close friend of your parents. Usually two names are chosen for you before you are born. Some parents would consult an astrologer on the suitability of the name or names they have chosen for their newborn baby.

For example, a girl from the East African coast might be called Amina (the trustworthy one); a boy might be called Amini, the male equivalent of the same name. This will be the name that you yourself will learn as a child and recognize, and to which you will respond. This name, along with the name of your father (and sometimes your grandfather as well) is your adult name, *jina la ukubwani*. Thus Amina's full name might be Amina Muhammed Salim - Amina the daughter of Muhammed, granddaughter of Salim. In some cases, she might be called Amina binti Muhammed bin Salim, Amina daughter of Muhammed son of Salim. This usage was much more widespread in the old days and is now used formally, as, for example, in passports or in marriage ceremonies! You will also meet this usage in Swahili literature. This is your legal name for the rest of your life.

WHEN IS THE NAME GIVEN TO YOU?

Immediately after your birth before you are shown the sun,[5] you are informed of your Creator's greatness by your father or a relative whispering into your ears, God is greater (*Allaahu akbar*). In the next breath you are told your name. Then you are introduced to the members of your immediate family and to their relatives and friends. They will wish to know what to call you and will ask what your name means if they are not already familiar with it. Your parents will then tell everybody your chosen name.[6]

If for some reason your parents have not decided in advance on your real name, that is, the name that you will grow with and use for the rest of your life, they will bestow on you a 'childhood' name, *jina la utotoni*. *Jina la utotoni*, this temporary name, is an affectionate kind of a nickname which might be chosen from such funny expressions as *kifimbo* (twig), *kigongo* (stick), *dodo* (beloved, or a name of a type of a mango large and round), *cheche* (mongoose, or a small part of whole), *mashavu* (cheeks), *panya* (mouse), *kidagaa* (sardine) *tatuni* (little one), *chiku* (chatterer), *tumbo* (stomach), *hobo* (gift), *doli* (doll), *chaki* (chocolate, dark brown) and so on. Two very common names are *sanura* (civet cat) and *paka* (cat). No child is ever called *Mbwa* (dog), since Waswahili consider dogs unclean.[7]

After the seventh day or when the child is forty days old (the numbers have ritual significance,) this name is changed to a permanent one, the *jina la ukubwani*. Some parents prefer to disclose their baby's proper name only after the seventh or fortieth day because they believe that announcing it sooner may harm the child. Sometimes, the two names may persist together, as in the case of Hemed Abdulla Kibao. Hemed (jina la ukubwani) Abdulla (father's name) Kibao (jina la utotoni).[8]

YOUR FAMILY NAME

The use of family names is not common in East Africa. Although family names have long been used by some people, as in the case of Hemed Abdulla Kibao Al-Ajjemy and earlier eighteenth century poets such as political theorist Muyaka bin Haji Al-Ghassaniy (1776-1840) and Muhyiddin bin Sheikh bin Abdi Sheikh Al-Qahtaany (1780-1869), the composer of a famous prayer for rain.[9] They were used only by certain groups of people. These people identified themselves by their full names along with tribal names such as Busaidi, Hinawi, Harthi, Kharusi, Kindi, Lamki, Mazrui, Riyami and the like. Family names often refer to a place of origin, a trade or profession, a nickname or if he were famous a great, great grandfather.

In recent times Waswahili who live in places such as

5

the Sultanate of Oman or the other Gulf states have been required to produce family names in order to establish their identity and heritage, to obtain citizenship rights and a legal passport. The use of surnames in the west is not a very old tradition either. In England it was only in the twelfth century that surnames began to come into use.[10] Family names have been quite common among the Arabs for a long time, real and fictitious, connecting an individual with some remote past.

THE MEANING OF A NAME

A name constructs a person. The name you carry may create an attitude in those who hear it even before they encounter you as a person. It also speaks to the dreams or expectations of those who named you. It will constantly remind you, in a symbolic way, of who you are to your parents and what you mean to them. It symbolizes a concept or idea to which you are held accountable. Since a name is so important, and carries so much meaning, Swahili parents like to give a child a name that has a favorable or praiseworthy meaning. Such a name will make a child think or act in a certain way. Choosing a good name is associated with a firmly held belief that a name is a reminder to a child of who he is, and so indirectly establishes his self-esteem.[11] A well known Swahili proverb declares: *Jina jema hung'aa gizani*, 'A good name shines in the dark.' The Swahili expression *Ni jina tu* 'It just a name' implies that the designated object does not stand up to the meaning of its name.

A name also expresses parents' expectations. You are what your name says you are, an honorable person, or a gentle or beautiful person or a brave or strong person.[12] As a child you are thus charged with the responsibility of acquiring, developing and maintaining the attribute that has been assigned to you through your name. When you fail to live up to your name, you will be reminded of its significance and so led to live up to its ideals. You may be reprimanded for spoiling your good name. In Kiswahili: *Unaharibu jina lako*, You are

are ruining your name. Those who are responsible in selecting one's name are in position of affecting or structuring the outcome.

THE CHOICE OF A NAME
The first girl in a family is often named after her grandmother on her father's side of the family, while a first-born boy is often named after his grandfather on his mother's side. The children who follow may take the names of other grandparents or other relatives, deceased or alive. Some people believe that when a child is named after another person he acquires his namesake's good and bad qualities.

A name may be chosen to depict the circumstances of a child's birth. It may allude to something that was happening at the time the child came into the world, or it may picture the baby's appearance at birth. Children born under difficult circumstances or those born in poor health may be called Shida (problem, stress), Tabu (difficulty), Mwatabu (child of difficulty), Sulubu (hardship), Uki (sadness).

There are also special names for a baby who is born with complications or who is not strong enough, or who has any form of defect or weakness. To ward off further misfortune such a child might be called Mwari (a god-child to someone), Mtumwa (a dependent or servant), Kijakazi (a maidservant) or Kitwana (a servant lad), implying that the child belongs not to the family alone but is also in the hands of his Creator. Some parents faced with a sick baby let a relative or a close friend take care of it, believing this will safeguard the baby's health. Names such as Mwari, Mtumwa or Kijakazi symbolize this arrangement.

Some names may indicate the actual moment that a child is born. The word Mosi means first. Thus if a child is called Mosi he may have been a first-born child or he may have been born on the first day of the week which in Swahili culture is Saturday (Jumamosi). Similarly a child called Pili (second) is named from the second day of the week, i.e

Jumapili (Sunday) or he may have been the second born. A girl called Tatu (third) would have been born on the third day of the week, Monday, Jumatatu, and so on. Tuesday is Jumaane and this is the name given to a boy; Machano is a boy born on Jumatano (Wednesday). Khamisi is a boy and Khamisuu a girl born on a Thursday, and Juma (and Mwana Juma) born on Friday, the last day of the Swahili week.[13]

Some names indicate the month in which a child is born, e.g. Rajabu, Shaaban, and Ramadhan. These are the three months that appear in the Islamic calendar as the seventh, eighth and ninth months, but in the Swahili calendar these are the tenth, eleventh and twelfth months. The name Ashur is given to a boy and Ashura to a girl born in 'the first ten days of the first month of the Islamic calendar', i.e. Muharram.

Sometimes a child is named after a season such as Masika or Vuli, the two rainy seasons in East Africa which occur from March to May and from November to December respectively. Sometimes a child is named after a significant calendrical event such as Idi or Mwanaidi. These are the two principle Muslim feast days which follow the fasting month of Ramadhan and the month of pilgrimage (the twelfth in the Muslim calendar). Maulidi is a name given to both boys and girls born during the month of the birth of the Prophet Muhammad, the sixth month of the Islamic calendar.

The name Arusi or Harusi signifies a child born at a time associated with an important family wedding just as Haji, Maka or Madina may signify a child born when a family member is making a pilgrimage to Mecca and Madina. The girl's name Mwaka signifies her birth during the Swahili New Year's celebration known by scholars as Nairuz. Comparable names in European Christian societies would be Natalie, Natallie or Natasha (for a girl born on Christmas day) or Pasquale or Pascal (for a boy born during Easter).

Sometimes a child's name may reveal the general nature of the relationship of her or his family with those around them when the child is born or immediately prior to

8

her or his birth. Such names include Siwatu (They are not behaving like good relatives, friends or neighbors), Siwazuri (They are not good), Chuki (Hatred), Haoniyao (S/he does not see his/her own fault), Sikudhani (I could not imagine such a thing) and Mtavila (You will eat it, your word, i.e. you will be sorry).

The name given to a child may also reveal the parents' philosophy or hopes as illustrated by the following names: Faraji (consolation), Masikini (poor), Riziki (providence), Shukuru (be grateful) and Subira (patience). Western names such as Hope, Charity, Joy, Patience, Prudence, Grace, Jane (gift of God), Jessica (God's grace) Olga (peace or holy), Amanda (loving), Vivian (lively), Andrea (brave), Alyson (a flower), Johanna, Joanne or Joan (grace/gift of God), Verona (truthful), Vincent (conquerer) and Amandina (worthy of love) express similar attributes, attitudes and expectations.

Muslim parents may choose as names for their children any of the ninety-nine attributes of God. These, it is believed, describe the knowledge, goodness and power of God and their use enhances the children to whom they are given as they use them in their daily lives. What the Qur'aan calls 'the Beautiful Names', al-asmaa' al-husnaa[14] include Al-'Aziim (the Great), Al-Baasit (the Extender), Al-Ghanii (the Self-Sufficient), Al-Qudduus (the Holy), Al-Hakiim (the Wise), Al-Jaliil (the Majestic), Al-Jabbaar (the Compeller, Powerful, Courageous) , Al-Kariim (the Generous) Al-Khaaliq (the Creator), Al-Qaadir (the Able), Al-Rahmaan (the Compassionate) Al-Rahiim (the Merciful), Al-Rauf (the Kind), Al-Samad (the Eternal), Al-Waduud (the Loving) and Al-Wahaab (the Bestower, Giver). When such names are used, they are preceded by the expression Abdu-l- Servant of). Thus, for example, a child is named Abdurrahmaan (the Servant of the Compassionate one), Abdulkhaaliq (the Servant of the Creator), Abduljabbaar (the Servant of the Courageous one), Abdulaziim (the Servant of the Great one) and so on.[15]

It is not considered appropriate for a Swahili parent

to name his son Aziim, Jabbaar or Khaaliq. To do so would denote arrogance and pomposity and would be considered sacrilegious. When, as in a few Muslim countries, such usage occurs, the name appears without the definite article, i.e. Aziim, (Great) but not Al-Aziim, (The Great).

Muslims may also give their sons some of the names of the twenty-five prophets whose names appear in the Qur'aan. Those used are Adam, Nuuh, Idriis, Ibraahiim, Isma'iil, Ishaaq, Ya'quub, Dauud, Sulaymaan, Ayyuub, Yuusuf, Muusaa, Haaruun, Ilyaas, Yuunus, Shu'ayb, Saalih, Zakariyya, Yahyaa, 'Isaa, and Muhammad. Some of these names may be abbreviated in speech. For example, the name Muhammad may be rendered Modi, Madi or Edi. Sulaymaan may become Selemani, Slemani or Suli. Abdulla may become Abdu or Dala or Dula.[16] Certain compounded names are also abbreviated, thus, for example, Mkamadume may become Makame and Mwinyi Mahdi may become Mwinyimadi.

Some girls' names are also shortened as, for example, Fatuma which may become Tuma or Fatma and Khadija which may become Dida. The names of famous Muslim women are frequently used for girls. These include Khadija, 'Aisha, Asma, Fatma, Maryam, Safiya, Khawla or Khola, Nasiiba, Lulu, Zubeida, Sabiha, Sauda, and Radhiya or Radiya.

THE SPELLING AND PRONUNCIATION OF NAMES

For a name to be understood within its semantic (meaning) boundaries, it has to fit the phonological (sound) structure of the language in order to be correctly pronounced and recognized. It is necesssary that the name one chooses be easy to articulate. Thus, regardless of any language from which the name might originally have come, for ease of pronunciation it is made to adapt to the Swahili sound system and to conform to its structure.

A name of Arabic origin, for instance, such as Faaḍil (abundance, excels) which appears in Arabic with ḍ, a velarized sound, is changed in Swahili to Fadhili pronounced with an interdental voiced dh. Similarly, Bakht (luck), will be changed to Bahati, Khayr (good) will become Kheri or Heri, Qamariyya (like a moon) will become Kamariya. Thus the Swahili sounds closest to them replace the original sounds.

Names with very unfamiliar sounds tend to be avoided. Thus no names in Swahili begin with C or X and only a few begin with the vowels O, U or E or the consonants P or V.[17] Certain combinations of sounds will sound foreign in Kiswahili and will be avoided. Names such as Mthinklulu, Mapfumo, Tapfuma and Ikechukwu, for instance, are never used in Swahili because they do not conform to Swahili syllable structure and are thus not appealing.

The same name with the same meaning may be pronounced differently, but only one pronunciation is adopted for the individual and used consistently by the parents. Hence a child may be named Rehema rather than Rahma, Amne instead of Amiina, and Fatuma instead of Fatma. Unintended pronunciations may be due to the nature of the spelling. Should for instance the name spelt as Malik be pronounced as Maalik, Maliik or Malik? These three are all possible pronunciations but only one relates to a particular individual. Similarly, Muhammad is variously written Mohammed, Muhammed, Mohamet and Muh'd; Abdalla is variously Abdulla, Abdullah or Abdula and Salim is variously Saleem or Saalim. It is vital to know how to pronounce a friend's name correctly so as not to arouse his displeasure.

Broadcasters often mispronounce names. For example, the name of Juma Ikanga, the New York Marathon runner from Tanzania, was mispronounced when he won the race in 1989. He was called Jama (pronouncing the phonetic /u/ as the sound in sun instead of its equivalent vowel sound in the word 'put'). In the broadcast commentary on the 1991 race, this was corrected. Another Swahili name Mzee (the title for the late president of Kenya, Jomo Kenyatta) is sometimes mispronounced Mzii. It should be pronounced Mzee as in 'say' in English.

In this book the Swahili conventional pronunciation

of a name is given along with any possible variants. As the main stress always falls on the next to the last syllable in Swahili, that vowel is always stressed and lengthened. The girl's name Khadija is thus always pronounced Khadeeja with the stress on the penultimate syllable.

The way a name is spelt may initiate a pronunciation that is different from its original.[18] Or the way a word is spelt may produce a different pronunciation from the intended one. We see this happening in names of Islamic origin in West Africa where, for example, the feminine suffix of the name Aminatu is pronounced whereas in Arabic the suffix is dropped and the name is simply given as Amina, and Khadijatu as Khadija the feminine suffix not being pronounced.

Although many variants of a name may exist, knowing its common pronunciation and its significance within the commmunity or culture to which it belongs is important. Very few people would recognize the Muslim philosophers Ibn Rushd (1126-1198) and Ibn Siinaa (980-1037) from their westernized names of Averroes and Avicenna respectively. Names are integral parts of any society's structure and a name not placed in its cultural context is like an empty shell washed up on a beach, lacking the content of meaning and the context of significance.

ADDRESSING ADULTS

A title is usually used when addressing an adult or someone older than you. It is judged disrespectful for a young person to address someone older than himself without prefixing Baba or Ba (Father), Bwana (Mr.), Baba mdogo or Mjomba (Uncle), Kaka (Brother), Mzee (Elderly) or Sheikh or Shekhe or She to his name. Sometimes you will use Sayyid (Mr.) and Mwalimu or Maalim (Teacher). If a woman is being addressed, the title of respect to be prefixed is Mwana or Nana (Lady), Mama or Ma (Mother), Bibi or Bi (Mrs. or Miss, Grandmother), Shangazi or Mama mdogo (Aunty) or Dada or Da (Sister).

In the olden days terms such as Fumo/Fume /Fuum/Mfaume/Mfalme (high, ruler), Makame (of high rank) Mtesa (shield, king) were also used.

When a child is named after a grandfather who is still alive, it is necessary to be respectful to the grandfather by referring to that child as Babu (Grandfather), Bwana Mkubwa (Big master), or Mwinyi (Ruler). This avoids using the grandfather's name without a title which is considered discourteous. Some Swahili children may refer to grown-ups not related to them as aunty or uncle, using the English expressions.

NAMES OF SIGNIFICANCE

Some names have lost their meanings or the meanings have been forgotten. However, their significance comes from the associations that they carry. Take, for instance, the name Maryam. Historically, in its Aramaic and Semitic form, marr, the word means bitter, signifying the treatment Maryam might have had. This name has also been identified by some scholar as of ancient Egyptian origin with the meaning "beloved". What ever its speculated origin this name is used today in its many variants all over the world with various phonetic forms, e.g. Mariyamu, Mariyama, Miriam, Mariyana, Maria, Mary, Marlene, Mae, Meiri, Meira, Mera, Mimi, Meye, and Molly among others. In this case, as with many other names, the original meaning of the name may not be known or may be disregarded, no importance being attached to it. Yet, of course, the name is very significant. Maryam or Mary represents the revered mother of Jesus Christ and is widely used in the Swahili community for this reason. Similarly, Khadija was the first wife of Prophet Muhammad. The name actually means 'premature' but this is beside the point. Both names are important to the Waswahili because of their connections, not because of their semantic meanings.

13

THE PERMANENCE OF A NAME

The name a child acquires usually remains with a person for life.[19] In the United States and many other western countries women usually take their husbands' names when they marry. This is not the case in East Africa. On marriage a Swahili woman is not required to change her name for that of her husband, although today some westernized Waswahili may choose to do so. However, even if a Swahili woman does take her husband's name, she does not drop her father's name but continues to use both names.

These days in western countries, a woman may choose to keep her family name but tag it onto her husband's name. Swahili women in their effort to westernize may well do the same one day in order to eliminate the ambiguity involved in using two different names for the same person. Until then, this use of two or more names may cause confusion for those who do not know current Swahili culture.

Understandablly, a woman's relatives and friends will refer to her by her father's name as a way of associating her with her father's lineage and affinity. Her more recently acquired friends and acquaintances may refer to her by her new name, her husband's. She may thus be identified both as Mrs. Aisha Zahran, using her father's name, as Mrs. Mansur, using her husband's name. She may also be known as Aisha using her own first name; or she may be named as the mother of her children, i.e. as Mama Fatuma or Mama Ali.

Once a Swahili child has acquired a name within the first forty days of birth, it is difficult to change that name. But some children lose their original names when they are brought up or adopted by others. This usually happens informally as there are no legal or ritual procedures involved in changing the name. Since a name is of great significance to a person, an individual who is deprived of his original name in this way when he is young, often reclaims it when he grows up.[20]

HOW NAMES REVEAL CULTURE

A name is a label that usually reveals membership in a group. A Swahili Muslim child will carry a Muslim name and is very unlikely to be called James or Jessica. However, there are cases of Muslim women being called, for example, Janet or Johanna, and Muslim men being called Robert or James.[21] This usage began during the colonial era in East Africa when parents needed to provide a child with a western education in private schools run by missionaries. Some missions, indeed, required that a child's name be changed. Another requirement was that school children should not use their native language.

Both phenomena, the change of name and dissociation from the Swahili language, are acts of cultural detachment and enforced alienation which destroy self-identity. In such a situation, where a Muslim carried a non-Muslim name, rumors about his identity might arise.[22] A typical case was that of the distinguished twentieth century Swahili poet, essayist, and novelist Shaaban Robert (1909-1962). His name is partly Muslim, Shaaban, and partly Christian, Robert, but because of his name Robert, his Muslim identity was obscured. Sheikh Shaaban composed a poem in Swahili to explain the confusion of his name.[23] In this poem which appears in his autobiography he clarifies his true and unfeigned identity. Declaring himself to be a true African, Shaaban Robert assures his readers that he is neither Arab, European nor Indian. Thus he writes:

Mwandishi ni Shaaban
Robert babangu miye.

Msidhani mahaluti,
Kabila sikusaliti,
Mwafrika madhubuti,
Vingine nisidhaniwe.

Sikuchanganya nasaba,
Kwa mama wala baba,
Ingawaje ni haiba,
Mimi sina asiliye.

Si Mwarabu si Mzungu,
Hindi si jadi yangu
Naarifu walimwengu,
Wadadisio wajue.

The writer is Shaaban,
Robert is my father.

Don't think that I am a mongrel
I am not of mixed blood
I am a true African
And should not be looked on otherwise.

My lineage is not mixed
On either my mother's or my father's side,
That is a privilege
I cannot claim.

I am neither an Arab nor a European,
I am not of Indian descent
I am letting everyone who questions
Know who I am.

So important to him was the question of names that
Shaaban Robert also wrote a second poem which he called
Jina, 'The Name'. If you are interested in reading it you will
find it in his book, *Pambo la Lugha*, published in 1966 by
Oxford University Press, Nairobi. In this poem Sheikh
Shaaban speaks about his reputation and prays to God for
the protection of his good name.

A different example of obscuring a name is that of
traditional women poets who concealed their real names and

used pseudonyms. We don't know exactly why they did this. The seventeenth century poetess who wrote 'Siri-li-asraar', a poem of five hundred and sixty-three stanzas of four lines each, completed in A.H. 1074 (1664 A.D.), identified herself as Mwana Mwarabu Binti Shekhe Bwana Lemba. This means 'An Arab woman, the daughter of Mr. Turban'. [24]

Another woman poet of a later period (1810-1860) refers to herself as Mwana Kupona, daughter of Msham. Her pseudonym means 'A woman who will recover'. Many other Swahili women poets have adopted pseudonyms. Some are to be found in today's East African daily newspapers. [25]

HOW NAMES REVEAL GENDER

Besides identifying the group identity of a person, many Swahili names reveal gender. Some Swahili names refer only to women. Examples include Farashuu, Moza, Fatma, Mize, Mboza and Rukiya. Names which are distinctively for men are Abdalla, Jecha, Muhammed, Ramadhani and Vuai.

A large number of names come in pairs and with small changes can be used for both males and females. This category includes such names as : Amin/Amina, Ali/Aliya, Aziz/Aziza, Aishi/Aisha, Ashur/Ashura, Fadhili/Fadhila, Fidel/Fidela, Adil/Adila, Harub/Harbiya, Khamisi/Khamisa or Khamisuu, Raashid/Rashida, Rais/Raisa, Saalim/Salma, Shariff/Sharifa, Shamsu/Shamsa, Samir/Samira, Zaki/Zakiya.

As we saw earlier when noting how babies could be named after the day on which they were born, in a few very rare cases a name may be used for both male and female. I can think of only eleven names not marked for gender: Maarifa, Majaliwa, Maulidi, Mgeni, Msiba, Mosi, Pili, Mwaka, Hindi, Nuru and Ubwa.

HOW NAMES REVEAL PARTICULAR SETTINGS

To be sure that one understands the meaning of a name, it is sometimes necessary to examine it within the particular context of the community in which it is used. The name a child bears reflects both his parents' language and their culture. It identifies a child as a member of a certain community. A name is culturally bound and linked to the language of the people so that they may appreciate and understand the meaning it holds.

The name Fujo, for example, has been said to mean 'She brings wholeness' in the Eastern Region of Africa.[26] Yet, in Kiswahili, Fujo would convey the opposite message,'confusion and disarray'. Swahili parents who live in East Africa are not likely to wish on their children such a trait. Another example, is the name Kesi which Asante says means 'Born when the father worked hard'.[27] In Kiswahili this name means to weigh, measure or judge and therefore represents a person who is an exemplar. It is always helpful to relate the name to the language and culture in which it is used in order to understand its message fully. Care has to be taken not to convey an unintended meaning.

Because names reflect the language and culture of the community in which they are given, there will be some which cannot be used universally to mean the same thing to everyone. Yet many nations as a result of historical and cultural contacts share a common experience, in spite of speaking different languages, and these, then, often have a fair number of names in common. This is true, for example, of Muslim Arabs, Bangladeshi, Persians (Farsis), Gambians, Hausas, Malaysians, Waswahili, Indians and Pakistanis, Yoruba and Senegalese. Since their common literary sources are the Qur'aan and the sunna ('traditions of the Prophet Muhammad') and their common religion is Islam, they have common sources of culture and knowledge.

18

FASHIONS IN NAMES

Traditional names persist in Swahili, constantly recurring as they are passed down from one generation to another. Hence among the men there are innumerable Abdallas, Muhammeds, Saalims, Saids and Jumas. As for girls, there is no shortage of Maryamus, Fatumas, Aishas, Salmas and Khadijas. Although grandparents pass down their names to their grandchildren, and uncles and aunts to their nephews and nieces, it is very rare to find children inheriting their parents' names (while they are alive). I have personally come across only one Musa bin Musa, i.e. Musa the son of Musa.

New and modern names keep surfacing all the time. These new names are acquired from neighboring countries, from name books, or from television and cinema. One important source for a new name is a spouse. Intermarriages bring fresh names. An Egyptian mother will introduce Egyptian names, and a Ugandan father Ugandan names. New names may also come about when parents have lived abroad. Names such as Fursiya, Firyaal, Firoza and Freni in one family may indicate a Persian connection. Katija, Zera, Zarina, Batuli and Alidina may suggest that one of the parents is of Indian ancestry. David, Kim, Amanda and Samantha suggest an English parent.

Some foreign names are adopted widely after their first appearance whereas others are phased out after a time. The name Johana, for example, in spite of its long existence in Zanzibar and its Afro-Asiatic connection (i.e. the root hanna, masculine, or hannat, feminine, meaning grace, compassion) is no longer widely used in Swahili East Africa. Natasha, on the other hand, (a child born on Christmas day) is a more recent adoption which, in spite of its historical and symbolic Christian meaning, is spreading. There is evidence of a long-standing fascination with names among the Waswahili and new names are introduced all the time. No formal research has yet been done to discover the principles behind the changing structure of nomenclature in this region yet clearly the changes come about in the historical course of events. These are reflected in a growing lexicon of Swahili children's names.

Very recently, for example, Waswahili who have emigrated to states in the Arabian Gulf have begun giving their children names derived from Arabic roots which were not found in East Africa in earlier times. It is too soon to assess whether these innovations will take in the different setting. It is, however, certain that, despite these recent fresh names appearing in the Waswahili diaspora, the general trend among the masses, both those abroad and those still living in East Africa, is to duplicate their relatives' names or to continue to use the historical and religious names long established in their communities.

POSITIVE AND NEGATIVE IDENTIFICATIONS

Not all names are given by the members of one language community. A name, when it is chosen by outsiders, may exalt a person or degrade him, or may in its historical perspective convey simply the attitude of its users towards that person or people. The designee may eventually accept the name regardless of its original connotation and will use it albeit in its new or secondary meaning.[28]

The word *Negro* continues to be defined as black in the recent etymological work of T.H.Hoad. In *Concise Oxford Dictionary of English Etymology,* he defines the word as black, black man, black moor, Spanish and Portuguese and repeats that the word negro is from Latin niger. Thus we may see that etymologists and others have long associated the English term negro with black although color was not its original meaning. They have also correlated black with degradation and humiliation. It takes time to correct long established etymologies even though alternative interpretations exist and even though there may be considerable interest among many people to do so!

Another good example is the term for a European or

any Anglo-Saxon person in Kiswahili. The name *Mzungu* which is derived from the Swahilisized Arabic word *zunduq* ' one who is not familiar with the Qur'an and so does not follow its obligations' becomes *-zungu* in Kiswahili. This original meaning of the word is now completely forgotten and has been superseded by a more favorable concept. Rev. Dr. Ludwig Krapf, defines *mzungu* in *A Dictionary of the Suahili Language*, London ,1882 as knowledge, skill, cleverness,..(p. 271). Johnson in 1939 in *A Standard Swahili-English Dictionary*, defines the word as 1. European 2. Something wonderful, startling, surprising, ingenuity, cleverness, a trick, a wonderful device etc.(p. 326). Many Swahili dictionaries adopt a similar definition. All convey a later interpretation rather than the original meaning.

There are several other negative labels that have been used to describe African people for instance, the use of the word *Berbers* in North Africa for the *Amazirg (Amasirh)* people. Their derogatory label 'barbary' which means those foreigners who do not speak properly which is derived from an innocent label *bar* 'land and in turn people of the land', has acquired a pejorative significance.[29] The concept and its label is better known today and used widely when referring to them than their original term of 'the free people or nomads'. Similarly, the term *hottentot* (huttentut) meaning "a quack" which was introduced by the Dutch, who did not understand their language, to refer to the African *Nama* and *Kora* who are among the *Lawu* (or Lawdhu), is better known than their original names.[30]

Words change their significance in time and place hence Swahili speakers should be aware of the contemptuous connotations of such labels as *boi* or *yaya* which they use to refer to their domestic workers. Nowadays, those sensitive to the derogatory meanings given these terms during the colonial era substitute *mtumishi* (one who serves) or *mfanyakazi, mfanyajikazi* (one who works). The label *boi* is obviously the English word for boy 'child' and to call a grown up man a boy degrades and indicates disrespect. As for the title *yaya* for a woman who works as a maid or a nanny, this might have been introduced to colonial East Africa from imperial India where the term *ayah* was used. An original derivation was probably from the Arabic vocative particle *yaa* which appears in front of a name when drawing someone's attention as to 'yaa Maryam,' 'Oh, Maryam'. In Kiswahili it is reduplicated and becomes yaya but it is used without the name. In Portuguese the word *aia* has a similar meaning of a maid, but since the term does not appear in other Romance languages its origin from Portuguese as claimed by some writers is doubtful. It is important to note that neither of these terms is itself derogatory in innocent, everyday usage. It is from the manner of their application and use that they indicate a lack of respect and degrade a fellow human being that is at issue. They contradict sensitive awareness.

Names of places have also led to negative perceptions. A graphic example is the image of Africa as a Dark Continent. Furthermore, its division into sub-Saharan Africa and Mediterranean Africa is arbitrary and may have political and racist overtones with Africa seen as a continent of white-skinned people in the north who are considered civilized and advanced while the rest of the continent is seen to be inhabited by black-skinned people considered backward, uncivilized and never travelled or participated in human civilization. This is a mispresentation as our meager documentation, archaeology and linguistic evidences suggest the opposite. The continent was known as *Afriqiyya/Ifriqiyya* from the root *firq* which meant dividing, separating, showing difference referring may be to the Mediterranean sea that separates this southern part of the world from the northern. This geographical term is not derived from Latin as some scholars have suggested and does not mean sunny or burnt faces as it has been claimed.

The fact that names have been used to identify people positively and negatively and sometimes to pass judgement about them, should still not be a barrier to unity or a cause for disunity. What creates injustice, intolerance, violence and bitterness among people is not their names, but their attitudes, their inability to acquire or attain the necessities of life -food, shelter, good health and education. The injustices that prevail are the issues that disregard and diminish moral values, and consequently weaken sensitivity towards others and cause rejection. But names themselves are not the cause of disunity and their cultural variety does not jeopardize Pan-Africanism or any other form of African unity. In fact, African names provide unity and a sense of common identity within multiracial and multicultural societies. To suggest that Africa should invent new names and abolish all names that are connected with gender and religion would not cure Africa's economic, political or social ills and, indeed, dangerously deflects from seeking real remedies for its problems.

The African continent is part of one world-system and was at the beginning a very important part of it. The Africans contribution to human civilization is now widely accepted.

Moreover trade between Asia and Africa dates back centuries to the pre- Christian era. Long before the First Egyptian dynasty, East Africans sailed the Azania ocean for trade and settlements. People of African descent contributed a great deal to both pre-Islamic culture and to the Islamic world and to the Arabic language. The prophet Muhammad is said to have had African blood and so was 'Antar ibn Shaddaad a pre-Islamic hero and poet of chivalry. Bilal ibn Rabaah was the dignified African who was the first muadhdhin (caller to prayers) in Madina. Zaid bin Abi Thaabit, a friend and adopted son of Prophet Muhammad and one of the six men who compiled the Qur'aan had an African origin. 'Uthman ibn 'Umaru Al-Bahr known as Al-Jahiz because of his large protruding eyes, was a famous ninth century writer of African descent in Iraq, who left us many celebrated Arabic literary works some of which have been translated into European and non-European languages. A millennium later, in the late nineteenth century, Sheikh Amadu Bamba of Senegal was writing in Arabic and his writings had great impact and are still being read and translated by his disciples, not only in Africa but other parts of the world as well. Their names Bilal, Thaabit, Othman, Omar, Ahmad, are common in East Africa today, yet their contribution to world civilization has not been sufficiently appreciated or recognized. [31]

In past centuries Islam, and the names derived from its culture, provided an early form of transnational or international unity. Over time Islamic civilization and culture spread throughout much of the world. Africa, Iran, India, Afghanistan, China, Malaysia, Indonesia, the Philippines and Russia, among peoples with very different languages and cultures. Arabic became an international language, just as Aramaic had been an international language before it, Latin after it, and English is today. Africa's contribution to Islamic language and culture is immense. The impact of Islam and of Arabic language and script on the world's languages and cultures is, in turn, extensive.

Swahili names constitute metaphors and are part of an oral and literary tradition that has grown up over many centuries. They are the sources of proverbial expressions and convey characterization in stories and dramas. In East African literature this technique of using names to capture metaphorically whole worlds of reality in symbolic expression goes back to traditional African folktales.

Among modern East African writers who have most successfully utilized the technique of capturing the image they wish to express through a name is Ebrahim Hussein.[32] Two of the leading women characters in his play *Wakati Ukuta* (Time is a Wall) are named Pili and Tatu and this is critical for understanding their relationships with Swai, the chief male character in the play. Similarly, the poet Hasani bin Ismail calls the medicine-man, the main character in his epic poem, *Nguvumali* (Power is wealth). The rest of the characters in his poetic narrative also carry symbolic names which reflect their relationships to each other and their roles. Thus, symbolically they are named Binti Ramadhani, Binti Jizi, Binti Hanifu, Salima, Yasinikimina, Shambi bin Dima and Ali. Any reader who does not grasp the meanings of their names cannot fully understand the message the poet is conveying or see how these named characters contribute to it.[33]

Historically, the significance and the power of names has been recognized and confirmed by secular and religious intellectuals alike. If one is persistently called a devil or a fool he eventually believes himself to be one. Names remind us of the past but they also alert us to the present. As Henry Thoreau once said, with knowledge of the name comes a distinctive recognition and knowledge of the thing. Six centuries before Thoreau, Sufi master and poet Jalal al-Din Rumi, born in the year A.H. 604/A.D.1207 in what today is Afghanistan, contended that a name is identical with the named.[34]

SWAHILI NAMES IN THE UNITED STATES

In the United States of America the last three decades of a renewal of black consciousness and African identity have introduced not just African history and culture, African dance, music, clothes and jewelry, African languages and literature, but African names. Many American children today are growing up with African names. Some are Swahili names and some are names from West African languages. This is one way in which the African-American community is asserting its African identity and raising its social consciousness. [35]

Following are some of the names I have heard used in the United States which have their origin or equivalents in Swahili personal names and the Swahili language. Those which are of Islamic origin are, of course, common not only to the Waswahili but to all Muslim peoples throughout Africa which is part of the world. You (the reader) may be familiar with other names that are not listed here.

FEMALE NAMES:

Adila ('aadilah)	just, upright
Afiya ('Affiah)	health
Afrika	Africa
Afua	healing, benefit
Aisha (Ayesha)	life
Amira	princess
Aneesa	companion
Aziza	precious
Bayyina	evidence, proof
Dhakiya	intelligent
Durah	pearl

Farida	unique
Fasaha	eloquence
Habeebah	dear one
Halima	gentle
Hamida	gracious
Hanifa	pure
Imara	firm
Imani	faith
Jamila (Gamilah)	beautiful
Janna	heaven
Jasira (Gasira)	bold, courageous
Jauhar	jewel

Khadejah (Khadija)	prophet Muhammad's first wife
Latifah (Latifa)	gentle
Maisha	life
Malaika	angel
Malaki	angel
Malika	queen
Malikia	queen
Manga	emigrant
Mema	goodness
Mila	traditions
Mimi	I am, or abbreviation of Maryam or Miryam
Mkweli	truthful
Mosi	first
Muslima	a Muslim, one who submits to God

Nadia	caller
Nadhari	vision, perception
Nafisa	precious
Nathari	prose, dispersion
Nena	speak
Nia	intention, purpose
Nina	lady
Penda	like, admire
Pendo	love
Pili	second
Rashida	intelligent
Rehema	compassion
Sabra	patience
Safiya	purity
Sakina	tranquility, calm

Salama	peaceful
Salima	safe
Salome	safe
Sanaa	art
Shahida	witness, martyr
Sharifa	honorable
Shida	difficulty
Siyasa	politics
Tabitha (Tabita)	graceful gazelle
Time	full of happiness
Tumaini	hope

Zahra	beautiful flower
Zaida	abundance
Zainab	Prophet Muhammad's daughter
Zakiya	pure
Zamani	long time ago
Zaynab/Zenabu	beautiful
Zawadi	gift
Zubayda	the best
Zuhura	brightness, Venus

MALE NAMES:

Abdul	Servant of the lord
Abdulhamid	Servant of the praiseworthy
Abdullatif	Servant of the kind one
Abduljabbaar	Servant of the brave one
Abdulmalik	Servant of the king
Abdulqudduus	Servant of the most Holy
Abdulrazzaaq	Servant of the provider
Abubakar	The first Khalifa after Prophet Muhammad
Adam	first human being ; first Muslim prophet
Ahmed	more commendable
Akili	mind, intelligence
Ali(Ally)	elevated
Al-farid Salahuddin	the unique religious reformer
Amani	peace
Amiri	prince
Antar	hero
Anwar	light, more light
Arif ('Arif)	knowledgeable
Asad	lion
As'ad	happier, more fortunate

Babu	grandfather
Baraka	blessings
Bilaal	the African voice that called out to Muslims to pray to one God;
Dagan (Dajan)	dark sky during a heavy rain
Damu	blood
Daud	David
Dhoruba	storm

Faqihi	wise
Fariid	unique
Furaha	happiness
Ghaniy	rich
Hafiz	guardian
Haki	right, justice
Hakim	judge
Hali	condition, state
Harambe	let's pull together
Hasani	good
Hasan	good
Hatari	danger
Hisham	generous
Hodari	smart, expert
Huseni	good
Idi Amin	festive and trustworthy, ex-president of Uganda
Iman	faith
Isma'iil (Ismail)	Ishmael, he hears

Jabali	strong as a rock
Jabir	restorer
Jalil (Jaleel)	exalted, honorable
Jamal (Jamaal)	elegance
Jamili (Jamiil)	handsome
Jauhar	jewel, gem
JituJeusi	big black man
Juma	born on Friday
Kafil	protector, responsible
Kamil	perfect
Kareem (Karim)	generous

Khabiri	aware
Khalid	vigorous
Kheri	goodness
Kinda	young bird, chick, young and beautiful
Kunjufu	cheerful
Kuumba	creativity, create
Kwanza	beginning
Kweli	truth

Lumumba	gifted
Madhubuti	firm, steady
Makamu	dignified
Malik (Maliki)	king
Maulana	our master
Mchawi	magician
Muhammad	praised, commendable
Musa	moses, powerful
Mustafa	chosen one, Prophet Muhammad
Mtembezi	one who roams about, a playboy
Mwanga	light
Mwanza	name of a town in Tanzania, beginner

Nathari	prose, embroidery
Niamoja	one purpose
Nuuh (Noah)	prophet, consolation
Omar	Khalifa, firm, better
Rashad	righteous
Rasul	messenger
Sabir	patient
Saidi	happy
Shaheed	witness, martyr
Shinda	overcome
Simama	stand up
Sulaymaan (Solomon)	Prophet, peaceful
Sultan	ruler, authority
Tariq (Taariq)	North African conquerer of Iberia (Andalusia) in 711. His name is given to Gibraltar (Jabal Taariq)
Tippu Tip	A famous nineteenth century Swahilit trader, he who blinks
Umoja	unity
Wakili	trustee, attorney,
Weusi	black
Yahya	John, living
Yusuf	Joseph

Some of these names are from the existing general inventories of universal Islamic and non-Islamic names. Others such as Fasaha, Nia, Sanaa Damu, Dhoruba, Harambe, Hodari, Kuumba, Kunjufu, Kweli, Haki, Madhubuti, Mchawi, Mtembezi, Jitu Jeusi, Simama, Uhuru are original innovations. They exemplify the use of the Swahili language by African-Americans to express their own messages establishing a new African-American culture. The messages inherent in these names portray African-Americans' consciousness and identity.

Most of the new Swahili names convey positive signals that are intended to praise and exalt a child or person not to degrade, denigrate, defame or disparage him. They establish a certain outlook, certain African traits, and they communicate a political or a social message. Many of these names first appeared in the 1960s and 1970s when African-Americans were actively working to change the image and feelings of the 'Negro' to that of a Black American or an African-American. It was at this time that Swahili names that signified their bearer was intelligent, responsible, steadfast, eloquent or powerful became popular.[36] In the idiom of the time he or she was black and beautiful. As in Swahili culture, the bearer of the name assumed the responsibility of living up to the meaning of the name.

African-American[37] cultural innovation and reconstruction in order to reclaim their heritage and make it meaningful and exemplary is also to be found in the terminology of Kwanzaa, the holiday celebrated between December 26 and January 1st.[38] The seven principles of the holiday all bear Swahili appellations. These are : umoja (unity), kujichagulia (self-determination), ujima (collective responsibility and work), ujamaa (cooperative economics), nia (purpose), kuumba (creativity), and imani (faith). This holiday, like the giving of Swahili names, is part of the African-American effort to create a positive and significant image for their community.

Names, indeed, convey the several identities each of

us has. Thus an African-American publisher by the name of Babatunde Khalid Shabaz Abdullah, asks and affirms:

What's in a Name? For those of us who have connected our life line to our past, it is culture, heritage, dignity, pride, strength, the love of self, the knowledge of self and most of all our beginning.[39]

In a nutshell, something exists only when it has a name.

There may be many different reasons why names are given but all have significance. They designate, describe and identify. Names are symbols that tell us who we are and what we may strive to be. They have been in existence since the birth of man - as the Swahili name Adam signifies - and they engender our view of ourselves and our behavior towards others.

Adam is the eternal man, the leader and father of humankind, and it seems only right that the name appears in so many cultures and languages, African and non-African, Christian and non-Christian, Muslim and non-Muslim alike. The name establishes a connection among them, an implication of at least a reference point if not a common bond. Adam stands for the ideal, if not yet the reality, that human beings who are created equal may yet live with dignity on the same earth even though they may be of different race, color or religion, one from the other.

PART TWO:
Swahili Names and Their Meanings

PART TWO:
Swahili Names and Their Meanings

MAJINA YA KIKE	FEMALE NAMES
Name	**Meaning**

Abla ('abla)	a wild rose
Adhra ('adhra)	apology
Adila ('adilia)	just, fair
Adla ('adla)	justice
Afaafa ('afaaf)	virtue
Afifa ('afifa)	virtuous, pure
Afiya ('aafiya)	health
Afua ('afwa)	forgiveness
Aida ('aaida)	gain, advantage
Aisha ('aaisha)	alive
Ajla ('ajla)	quick, fast
Alama ('alama)	sign
Aliya ('aliya)	exalted

Amali	hope
Amana	trust
Amina	trustworthy, faithful
Amira	princess
Amne	secure
Amra	lasting power
Anisa	friendly
Anisun	friendly
Arafa ('arafa)	knowledgeable
Arifa ('arifa)	knowledgeable
Arusi (Harusi)	wedding
Asatira	legend, saga
Asha ('aasha)	living

Ashura ('ashuura)	companion, born in the first ten days of the Islamic new year.
Asila (Asiila)	noble origin
Asiya	console
Asma	higher, more exalted
Asmahani	exalted
Asumini	jasmine
Atiya ('atiya)	gift
Awena	gentle
Aza ('azza)	powerful
Aziza ('aziiza)	precious

B

Badriya	moonlike
Bahati	luck
Bahiya	beautiful
Barke	blessings
Basha	act of God
Bashaam (Bashshaan)	rich
Bashira	predictor of good news
Basma	a smile
Batuuli	maiden
Baya	ugly
Bebi	baby
Bia	home, environment
Bilqisi	queen of Saba'a, Shibaa
Bimbaya	ugly lady
Bimdogo	young lady
Bimkubwa	older lady
Bimnono	fat lady
Bishara	good news
Bitisururu	daughter of happiness
Bititi	strong lady
Biubwa	baby-like, soft and smooth
Bushira (Bushra)	announcer of good news

Chausiku   born at night
Cheche   small thing
Chiku   chatterer
Chinjo   slaughter, cut
Chipe   sprout
Chuki   dislike, resentment

Dalali   broker
Dalila   sign, proof
Dawa   medicine
Dhambizao   the sins are their's
Dhuriya   descendant
Dodo   lovable, large and round
Doli   doll
Doto   one of the twins
Ducha   little
Duni   small
Durra (Durah)   large pearl

Eshe   life

F

Fadhiila (Fadila)	outstanding, abundance
Fadiya	redeemer
Fahima	learned, understands
Faida	benefit
Faika (Faiqa)	superior
Faiza	victorious
Fakhta	pierce
Farashuu	butterfly
Farida	unique
Fathiya	triumph
Fatuma (Fatma)	Prophet Muhammad's daughter

Fauziya	successful
Feruzi	turquoise
Fidela	feminine of Fidel, faithful
Fila	badness
Firdawsi	paradise, beautiful garden

Firyali	extraordinary
Freya	godess of love, Friday
Furaha	happiness
Fursiya	heroism

Ghalye/a	expensive, precious
Ghaniya	rich
Gharibuu	stranger, visitor

Habiba (Ḥabiba)	beloved
Hadiya (Hediye)	gift
Hafidha	mindful
Hafsa	sound judgment, Prophet Muhammad's wife
Haifa	slim
Hakima (Ḥakiima)	sensible
Hala	glorious
Halima (Ḥaliima)	gentle
Hamida (Ḥamiida)	appreciative, glorifies
Hanaa	happiness
Hanifa (Ḥaniifa)	pure
Hanuni	cheerful
Haoniyao	self-righteous
Harbuu (Ḥarbuu)	warrior
Hartha (Ḥartha)	arable, fertile
Hasanati (Ḥasanaat)	merits
Hasiina (Ḥasiina)	beautiful, attractive

Hasnaa (Ḥasnaa)	beauty
Hawa (Ḥawaa)	mother of humankind
Hayati (Ḥayaat)	life
Hiba	gift
Hindi	Indian, sharp armor
Hobo	gift
Horera	kitten
Huda	guidance
Hudham	astute
Hujayja	evidence
Husna (Ḥusna)	most beautiful

Ibtisam	smile
Iffat ('iffat)	virtue
Ilham	inspiration
Imani (Imaan)	faith
Inaya ('inaya)	providence
Intisar(Intiṣaar)	victory
Itidal (I'tidaal	symmetry

Jaha	prominence
Jahi	prominence
Jahia	prominent
Jamila	beautiful
Jina	name, identity
Johanna	God's grace
Jokha	embroidered brocade
Judhar	uproot
Juwayria	damask rose
Juza	notify

Kalolii	feeble
Kamaria	moon-like
Kamilya	perfection
Karima	generous
Kashore	smiles
Kaukab	star
Kauthar	abundant
Kazija	plenty of work
Kesi	exemplar
Khadija (Hadija)	Prophet Muhammad's first wife
Khanfura	snort
Khola (Khawla)	deer

Kibibi	young lady
Kidawa	medicine
Kifimbo	stick
Kijakazi	young maid
Kijicho	envious
Kujuwakwangu	my knowing
Kurwa	repetition, second of twins

Lamia (Laami'a)	glitter
Latifa(Laṭiifa)	gentle
Layla	night
Lela	night
Lila	good
Lubaya	young lioness
Lubna	storax
Lulu	pearl
Lyutha	the wealthy

Maarifa (Ma'rifa)	experience
Maasuma (M'asuuma)	impeccable
Maatuka (Ma'tuuqa)	emancipated
Machui	leapord like
Madiha (Madiiha)	praiseworthy

Mae (Mai)	a variant of Maryam, Mary and May
Mafunda	instruction, training
Mahbuba (Mahbuuba)	beloved
Mahfudha(Mahfuuza)	protected
Maka	Mecca
Maliha (Maliiha)	pleasant
Malika (Maliika)	queen
Mariamu (Maryam)	Mary
Marjani	coral
Masara	happiness
Mashavu	cheeks
Masika	rainy season
Maskini	poor, humble
Mastura	protected from blemish, well-covered
Mathna	extol, praise, appreciative
Matima	full moon
Maua	flowers
Maulidi	birthday of prophet Muhammad
Mayasa	walks proudly
Maymuna	blessed
Maysara	ease
Mboza	sulky, a type of a tree
Menkaliya	from Mmenikaliya, you are against me
Mera	a variant of Maryaam and Marie and May
Meyyaan	not a real friend or the dual of Meyya. See next entry.
Meyye (Meyya)	a variant of Maryam, Mae, Maie
Mgeni	visitor
Mkali	fierce
Mkiyoni	from Hamkiyoni, you don't see it
Mmanga	a trip,journey from Oman, emigrant
Mosi	first

Moza	distinguished
Mrashi	rose water sprinkler
Mshinda	successful
Msiba	grief
Mtakuja	you will come
Mtakwishayenu	you will exhaust your tricks
Mtama	millet
Mtumwa	messenger, servant
Mufiida	beneficial
Muhima	important
Muna	hope
Munira	radiant
Mvita	full of life
Mwajuma	born on Friday

Mwaka	born in new year
Mwamini	believer
Mwammoja	only one, first one
Mwana	lady
Mwanabaraka	brings blessings
Mwanadongo	earthy, child of the land
Mwanahamisi	born on Thursday
Mwanahawa	daughter of Hawa, mother of humankind
Mwanaidi	born on Idd day, i.e. Muslim Holy day
Mwanakhamisi	born on Thursday
Mwanakheri	brings goodness
Mwanakweli	brings truth
Mwanamize	distinguished
Mwari	a girl who has reached puberty

Mwasaa	timely
Mwasham	unlucky
Mwatabu	person of difficulty
Mwema	good

Nabila	noble
Nadhira (Naziira)	foremost
Nadiya	generous
Nadra	scarce
Nafisa	priceless, gem
Nafla	gift
Naima (Na'iima)	graceful
Najaat	safety
Najah (Najaah)	success
Najla (Nagla)	progeny
Najma	star
Najya	saved
Nana	lady
Nargisi	narcissus
Nasiim	fresh air
Nasra	assistance
Natasa	skillful
Natasha	variant of Natalia
Nayfa	benefit
Nayla	gain

Naysun	dangling seedless grapes
Neema (Ne'ma)	bounty

Nina	mother
Nisriin	wild rose
Nuha	consoled
Nunuu (Nunu)	extol
Nura	brightness
Nuru	light
Nuzha	pleasure
Nyimbo	song

 P

Paka	cat
Panya	mouse
Pili	second

 R

Raawiya	story teller, deliberation
Rabia (Rabi'a)	spring
Rabuwa	grow
Radhiya(Raziya)	contented

Rafiya	dignified
Rahima(Rahiima)	compassionate
Rahma (Rahma)	compassion
Raisa	president
Ramla	divination
Rashiida	righteous
Rayha	small comfort
Rayyan	luxuriant, lush
Razina	strong and patient
Reem (Rim)	white antelope
Rehema	compassion
Riziki	sustenance, fortune
Rozi	flower, rose
Rukiya (Ruqaya)	superior, Prophet Muhammad's daughter
Ruzuna	calm, composed

Saada	happiness
Saadiya(Sa'adiyya)	happy
Sabiha (Sabiiha)	beautiful, graceful
Safaa (Safaa)	purity, clearness
Safiya (Safiyya)	clear, pure
Saida (Sa'iida)	happy
Sakina(Sukaina)	quiet
Salama	peace
Salamuu	safe
Salha (Salha)	good
Salima	safe
Salma	safe
Salme	safe
Salwa	consolation
Samiha (Samiha)	magnanimous
Samira	reconciler

Sanura	civet cat
Sara (Sarah)	joyful
Sauda	black, Prophet Muhammad's wife, lady
Saumu (Ṣaumu)	fasting, born during the month of Ramadan
Sauti	voice
Sebtuu	born on Saturday
Semeni	speak
Shafiiqa	kind-hearted
Shahrazad	princess
Shakila	well-shaped
Shamba	plantation, branches
Shamim	sweet scent
Shangwe	celebration
Shani	circumstance
Sharifa	noble
Shawana	grace
Shemsa	sunlight
Shiba	satiated
Shifaa	cure
Shukuru	grateful
Shuruku (Shuruuq)	dawn
Sibadili	I will not change
Sihaba	not a little
Siham	sharing, participation
Sijaona	I have not seen
Sikitu	it's all right, it's nothing
Sikudhani	I never thought
Siti	lady

Siwatu	they are not people
Siwazuri	they are not good people
Siyasa	politics
Somo	instruction, godmother
Somoe	her godmother
Staajabu	surprised
Stara	well-covered, protected
Subira (Subra)	patience
Suhaila	ease
Sultana (Sultaana)	ruler
Suluma	security
Sumaiyya	of good reputation, high
Surayya	noble

Taabu	difficulty
Taanisa	sociable
Tabasamu	smile, happiness
Tabia (Tabi'a)	habit
Tabitha, Tabita	graceful
Tafida	benefit
Tahira(Tahira)	clean
Tahiya (Tahiyya)	security
Talha(Talha)	easy life
Tamaa	desire, ambition, greed
Tanabahi	be cautious
Tathmina	high value
Tatu	three
Tausi (Tausi)	peacock
Tawilu (Tawiilu)	tall
Taymura	guardian
Tefle (Teflah)	infancy, beginning

Thurayya	Pleiades
Thuwayba	small gift
Time	high, full of happiness
Tufaha (Tufaaha)	apple
Tuhfa (Tuhfa)	gift
Tuni	tune
Tunu	novelty
Turkiya	beautiful

Umayma	young mother
Umi (Ummi)	my mother
Ummkulthum	Prophet Muhammad's daughter
Umsa'ad	happy mother
Unguja	Zanzibar

Yasmin	jasmine
Yathriba	old name for Madina
Yumna	good luck, happiness
Yusra	ease
Yuuthar	wealthy, plentiful

Wafaa	long life, accomplishment
Wahiba	gift
Walyam (William)	protector

Zaafarani	saffron
Zahra	flower
Zaina	beautiful
Zainab	Prophet Muhammad's daughter
Zaituni	olive, guava
Zakiya	pure, righteous, excellent
Zalika	well-born
Zamzam	holy spring
Zarifa	graceful
Zarina	golden
Zawadi	gift
Zena	beautiful ornament
Zera	beauty, blooms, dawn
Zeyana	ornament
Zina	beauty
Zubeda	cream of the crop, Harun Rashid's wife, best
Zuhura	brightness, beauty, Venus
Zulekha, Zulaykha	brilliant, ahead
Zuwena	small and beautiful

MAJINA YA KIUME MALE NAMES

NAME   **MEANING**

Abasi ('abbaas)	stern, Prophet Muhammad's uncle
Abdu ('Abdi)	servant of God
Abdalla	servant of God
Abdulaziz	servant of the dear one
Abdulbasit	servant of the extender
Abdulghaffaar	servant of the forgiver
Abdulghaffuur	servant of the forgiving
Abdulghani	servant of the prosperous
Abdulhaliim	servant of the clement
Abdulhamiid	servant of the praiseworthy
Abduljaliil	servant of the majestic
Abdulkarim	servant of the bountiful
Abdulkhaliq	servant of the creator

Abdulla	servant of God
Abdullahi (Abdillah)	servant of God
Abdullatiif	servant of the gracious
Abdulmajiid	servant of the glorious
Abdulmu'ti	servant of the doner
Abdulnassar	servant of the savior
Abdulqaadir	servant of the able
Abdulwahhab	servant of the bestower
Abdulwaahid	servant of the one
Abdulwahiid	servant of the unique

Abdulwakiil	servant of the trustee
Abdurrahim	servant of the merciful
Abdurrahman	servant of the beneficent
Abdurrasul	servant of the messenger
Abdurrauf	servant of the compassionate
Abdussamad	servant of the eternal
Abedi	worshiper
Abubakar	first Khalifa after the death of Prophet Muhammad
Abudu/Aboud	servant of God
Abuu	father
Adamu (Adam)	first human being
Adil ('adil)	just
Adnan('adnaan)	good fortune
Ahmed; Ahmada	more commendable
Akbar	greater
Akida ('aqiida)	belief
Akili ('aqiil)	intelligence, mind
Akram	more generous
Alamini	trustworthy
Alhaadi	guide
Ali ('ali)	exalted
Amaad ('amaad)	support
Amani	safety
Amar ('amar)	long life
Ambar ('ambbar)	ambergris
Ame ('amm)	universal
Amini	trustworthy
Amiri	prince
Amran ('amraan)	prosperity
Anasa	entertainment
Antar ('antar)	hero
Anwar	bright
Arif ('aarif)	knowledgeable
Asani ('assaan)	rebellious
Asante	you have been good, thank you

Asghar (Asghar)	younger
Ashraf	more noble
Ashur ('aashuur)	born in the first ten days of Muharram
Athumani('uthmaan)	third Khalifa
Atif ('aatif)	compassionate
Ayubu (Ayyub)	Job
Azaan ('azzaan)	strength
Aziz ('aziiz)	precious

Baakir	eldest, early
Baba	father
Babechi	father echi
Babu	grandfather
Badawi	nomad
Badilini	change
Badrani	moon-like
Badru	full moon
Baha	brilliance
Baka (Baqaa)	permanence or abbreviation of Bakari
Bakari	shortened from Abubakr, first- born
Baraka	mystical blessings
Barghash	Sultan of Zanzibar (1870-1888), gnat
Bashiri	predictor
Bausi	sharpener of knives
Bavuai	fisherman

Bilali	first muadhdhin (Muslim caller for prayer), stood a test
Boma	fortress
Boraafya	better health
Burhaan (Burhani)	proof
Bushiri	predictor

C / Ch

Chacha	strong
Chaga (Chega, Cheja)	holiday
Chandu	octopus
Chimaisi	young and proud
Chum	black
Chuma	iron, strong

Dahoma	long life
Daraja	bridge, stage
Darweshi	dervish
Dau	abbreviation of Daudi
Daudi	David
Dogo	small
Dude	what'chma callit

Fadhili (Fadil)	virtuous
Fahim	learned
Faki	hollow, simple, or abbreviation of Fakihi
Fakihi (Faqiih)	wise
Fakhri	glory, honor
Faraji	consolation
Farhani (Farhaan)	happy
Farid	unique
Farjalla	God's consolation
Faruki (Faruuq)	judicious
Fathi (Fathi)	victorious
Fauzi	successful
Fehed	lynx, panther
Feisal	arbitrator
Feruzi	turquoise
Fidel	faithful
Fikirini	reflect
Fogo	high
Fuad	heart
Fumu (Fumo)	majesty
Fundikira	learned
Funga	tie, bind
Furaha	happiness

G/Gh

Ghalib (Ghaalib)	winner
Gharib	stranger, visitor
Gheilani	type of tree

Haamid (Haamid)	grateful
Habib (Habiib)	beloved
Hafidh (Haafiz)	preserver
Haidar (Haidar)	strong, stout
Haji (Hajj)	pilgrim
Haki (Haqq)	right, truth
Hakim (Hakiim)	judge, wise
Hamadi	gracious
Hamdaan (Hamdaan)	praise
Hami	defend
Hamisi(Khamis)	born on Thursday
Hamza	Prophet Muhammad's uncle, strong
Hanif (Haniif)	resolute in belief
Harub (Haarub)	warrior
Haruun	messenger, Aharon, Aaron
Hasani (Hasan)	good
Hashil (Haashil)	emigrant
Hashim (Haashim)	honor
Hasnuu	handsome
Hauli	power, strength
Hilali (Hilaal)	crescent
Himidi	grateful
Hindi	Indian, sharp armor
Hishaam	generosity
Humud (Humuud)	gracious

Hurani	restive
Huseni (Husain)	diminutive of Hasan, good
Husni (Husni)	goodness

Ibrahim (Ibrahiim)	Ebrahim, Avraham
Idi	festivity
Idriis	prophet, he studies
Ilyaas	prophet Elijah, the Lord is my God
Imaad ('imaad)	pillar
Imaan	faith
Isa ('iisaa)	Jesus
Isaam ('isaam)	guard
Ishaaq	prophet, laughter
Islam	safe, submission to God
Isma'iil	prophet, he hears

Jaafar (Ja'far)	small river
Jabiri (Jaabir)	comforter
Jaha	dignified
Jalali	high, majesty
Jalili	exalted, dignified
Jamaadar	army general

Jamali (Jamaal)	beauty
Jamil	handsome
Jamshid	Persian king, Solomon, Jonas
Jawaad	generous
Jecha	sunrise
Jefar	recovery
Jelani	great
Jenebi	affectionate
Jengo	building, strength
Juma	born on Friday
Jumanne	born on Tuesday
Jumba	large building

Kamali	perfection
Kame	desolate
Kandoro	a type of sweet potato
Karama	generosity
Karim	generous
Karume	master
Kesi	judging, rational
Keto	depth
Khalafu (Khelefu)	succeed
Khalfan	successor
Khalid (Khaalid)	lasting
Khalifa	successor, viceroy
Khalil	sincere friend
Khalladi	lasting
Khamisi	born on Thursday, soldier in Prophet Muhammad's army
Khatibu; Khatib	orator
Khayralla	God's best
Kheri	goodness

Khiari	preference
Kiango	lampstand, light
Kibasila (Kibasira)	insight
Kibwana	young gentleman
Kibwe	blessed
Kifimbo	stick
Kigoma	small drum, joy
Kigongo	pole, stick, firm
Kim	abbreviation of Kimberley, diamond rock South African diamond mines
Kimameta	cloth
Kimweri	ruler, chief

Kinjeketile/Kinjikitile	he killed himself
Kipanga	falcon
Kisasi	revenge
Kitunda	small fruit
Kitunzi	reward
Kofi	handful
Kombo	impoverished, bent
Kondo	warrior
Kongoresi	old contest

L

Lali	flexible
Latif (Laṭiif)	gentle
Liyongo	talks nonsense
Lumumba	gifted

M

Maabade	sanctuary
Maalik	king, owner
Maarifa	experience
Maamuni	reliable
Mabruke	blessed
Majaliwa	destined
Majid/Maajid	innovator
Machano	born on Wednesday
Machungwa	orange season
Magoma	celebration
Mahbuub (Maḥbuub)	beloved
Mahdi	rightfully guided
Mahfuudh (Maḥfuuẓ)	preserved
Mahmud (Maḥmud)	praised
Majuto	regret
Makame	high rank, ruler
Makungu	initiation
Makwetu	our place
Maliik	king, owner
Maliki	king, owner
Mambo	matters, events
Mandara	leader

Maneno	words
Mansuur (Manṣuur)	protected
Manzi	residence
Mapute	empty, taken away
Marzuku (Marzuuq)	blessed
Mash'al	torch
Masud (Mas'uud)	fortunate
Matari (Maṭar)	rainy season
Matogo (Matojo)	markings on the face
Matwa	sensible
Maulidi	born in the month of Prophet Muhammad's birthday
Mbaarak (Mbaruku)	blessed
Mbamba	branch of a tree, thin
Mbaya	bad, ugly
Mbita	quiet
Mbogo	buffalo, spokesman

Mbwana	master
Mdahoma	long life
Mdogo	young
Mfaki	exalted
Mfaume	king
Mgeni	visitor
Mhina	comfort
Mirza	prince
Miujiza	miracle
Mkadam (Mqaddam)	ahead, leader
Mkamba	rope maker, a Kamba tribe person
Mkubwa	senior

Mosi	first
Mrehe (Mrekhe)	easy life
Msamaki	fisherman
Msellem	flawless
Mshabaha	resemblance
Mshangama	rising
Mtavila	you'll eat it
Mtoro	runaway
Mubaadar	undertakes
Mudrik	intelligent, reasonable
Mufid	beneficial
Muhamadi (Muhammed)	praised, commendable
Muhashmy	weak
Muhashsham	respected
Muhidini (Muḥyiddiin)	revivalist
Muhsin (Muḥsin)	beneficent
Muhyiddin	bestower of religion
Mukhtaar	chosen
Mundhir	sign, reminder
Munim (Mun'im)	benefactor
Muniir	shining
Muombwa	beseeched
Muraad	good intention
Murshid	guide
Murtadha (Murtada)	disciplined
Musa	Moses
Muslih (Musḷiḥ)	reformer
Muslim	submits to God peacefully

Mustafa (Mustafa)	well chosen
Muumin	believer
Muyaka	good and truthful
Mwalimu	teacher
Mwapacha	twin
Mwendapole	walks slowly, cautious
Mwinyi	ruler
Mwinyimadi	just ruler
Mwinyimkuu	great ruler
Mwita	caller
Mzale	native
Mzee	elderly

Naadir	rare
Naasir	defender
Nabhani	sensible, judicious
Nabil	noble
Nadhim	organizer
Najiib	noble
Nanji	safe
Nasila	honey
Nasiir	helper
Nasor	saved
Nguvumali	power is wealth
Nuuh (Nuuh)	Noah, consoled
Nuru (Nuur)	light
Nyuni	bird

| Omari ('Umar) | long life |

Pandu	artistic
Pili	second
Pongwa	cured
Popo	bat, sleeps in the daytime

Qaadir (Kadiri)	capable
Qaasim (Kaasim)	just
Qays (Kesi)	logical

Raashid (Rashidi)	pious
Raha (Raahaa)	comfort
Rahiim (Rahiim)	merciful
Rajabu	born in the eighth month (Islamic calendar)
Ramadhani (Ramadaan)	born in the Muslim month of fasting (cf. Saumu)
Rashaad	righteous
Rauf	kind, merciful

Rehani	sweet smell, basil, comfort
Rejalla (Rajaa'lla)	God's wish
Ridha (Ridaa)	contented
Ridhwani	consent
Rifai (Rifaa')	elevated
Rijaal pl.of Rijjaal/Rajul	man
Rubama	possibility
Rubanza	courageous
Rumaliza	deliverance

Sa'ad	good fortune
Saalim	safe
Saami	exalted
Saburi	patience
Sadiki	trustworthy
Safari	journey
Safwani	sincere
Saghiri	young
Sahalani	ease

Said (Sa'iid)	happy
Salaahuddin	improves religion
Salaam	peace
Salah (Salaah)	goodness
Saleh (Saalah)	good
Saliim	safe
Salmini	saved
Samiih (Samiih)	magnanimous

Samiir	companion
Sarahani (Sarḥaan)	free
Sefu (Seif)	sword, brave
Shaabani (Sha'baan)	ninth month
Shaafi	healer
Shaahid (Shahidi)	witness
Shahaab	shooting star
Shakwe	shoot up, growth, sprout
Shamakani	leader of the place
Shambe	leader
Shariif	noble
Shazidi	growth
Sheikh	leader, elder
Shilingi	shilling, money
Shinuni	attack
Shomari	type of a mango, long and thin
Shujaa	brave
Sikujua	I didn't know
Simba	lion
Sinaan	spearhead, brave
Songoro	smith
Stima	engine, ship
Sudi	good luck
Sulaiman (Selemani)	wise, Solomon
Sultaan	ruler
Sulubu	tough
Sululu	consolation
Sumai (Simai)	high
Sumait	reputable
Su'uud	good luck
Suwedi	young master
Suwesi	govern

Taahir (Taahir)	clean
Taalib	seeker of knowledge
Taghlib	overcome
Taha (Taaha)	the opening of the 20th sura in the Qur'aan, skillful
Taki (Taqi)	God-fearing
Tamiim	perfection
Tarik (Taariq)	visitor
Tawfiki (Tawfiiq)	divine guidance
Taymur	manager, defender
Thaabit	firm, steadfast
Thani	second one
Tharwat	power
Thayru/Thairu	rebellious, furious
Thuweni	diminutive of second thani
Tindo	active
Tumbo	stomach
Turki	handsome, beloved, planet

Ubwa	delicate, young
Uki	sadness, impediment
Uledi	young man
Umar ('Uma, Omar)	longevity, second Khalifa
Umbaya (Ubaya)	bad feeling
Usaama ('usamaa)	precious
Usi	hard
Uthman ('uthmaan)	third Khalifa

Vuai   fisherman

Waduud   companion
Wahid (Wahiid)   unique
Waiyaki   unto you
Wajihi   distinguished
Wakili   trustee, attorney
Waliid   new-born child, productive
Waziri   vizier, minister, advisor

Yaasiin (Yasini)   sura in the Qur'aan, rule, principle
Yaakubu (Ya'quub)   Jacob, James, Akub,
Yahya   lives, John
Yassir   ease
Yunus   Jonah
Yusuf   Joseph

Zahir (Zaahir)	shining
Zahor	blooming
Zahran	shine
Zaid	abundance
Zakariya	Zaccharias, rememberance
Zaki	virtuous
Zakwani	thriving
Zalika	born of good family
Zamoyoni	of the heart
Zende	forearm, strong and firm
Zuber	brave
Zuher	shining
Zuri (Zuhri)	good looking

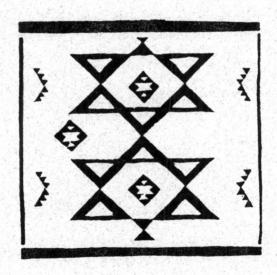

Footnotes

1. William Shakespeare, *Romeo and Juliet*, Act II Scene ii. Juliet is talking to Romeo about his family name, Montague. The sentence has since captured the attention of many writers interested in names.

2. The most recent is *The Book of African Names* by Molefi Kete Asante, Africa World Press, 1991. Others include: Keith Baird, *African Names;* Dawuud Hakim, *Arabic Names and Other African Names with Their Meanings,* Hakim's Publications,1970; Nia Damali, *Golden Names for an African People,* Blackwood Press, 1986; Moulana Ahmed Muhammad Hathurani, *Names For Muslim Children,* Dawah Book Shop,(n.d.) and Louise Crane, *African Names: People and Places,* University of Illinois, 1982. The subject of names has fascinated many American psychologists and others who have compiled books and formulated theories on the influence of names on individuals. This book deals only with the meanings and usage of Swahili names and not with their likely or supposed behavioral effects.

3. In their *Dictionary of Word and Phrase Origins,* the Morrises relate 'name' to the Latin nomen, Old English nama, Germanic, namon, Gothic name, and Sanskrit naama.

4. The word s-m in both Arabic and Swahili means also

poison. This association of meanings may have something to do with the superstition.

5. The Swahili word for sun is jua which also means the verb to know. On the one hand seeing the sun is exposing one to the light and at the same time knowledge. On the other hand knowledge is seeing light.

6. Alex Haley in *Roots* in 1976, gave an account of Kunta's family in which he described the naming ceremony of a new-born child which takes place on the eighth day (p.2). This ritual takes place in West Africa, on the opposite side of the continent, but it bears a close resemblance to naming rites on the East African coast. The book has now been translated into Swahili with the title *Asili*. This is Swahili for 'Origin', i.e. 'Roots'. Some societies where names are not gender specific name the child before it is born.

7. In ancient China children were given ugly names to keep away the evil spirits. Others conceal the real name and use a nickname for similar reasons.

8. Hemed Abdulla Kibao was a famous Swahili author. He wrote *Wakilindi* (The Kilindi) (Boston University Press, 1963) and three famous Swahili epics: *Utenzi wa Abdirrahmani Na Sufiyani: The History Abdurrahman*, (East African Literature Bureau, 1961); *Utenzi Wa Seyyidna Huseni Bin Ali:The History Of Prince Husein Son of Ali (East African Literature Bureau, 1965) and Utenzi Wa Vita vya Wadachi Kutamalaki Mrima, (The German Conquest of Tanganyika)*. His nickname, Kibao, means a piece of wood, a stool. He is also known in the academic world by his family name, Al-Ajjemy.

9. The family name of Muyaka appears in *Diwani ya Muyaka bin Haji Al-Ghassaniy (Swahili Poems of Muyaka)* ed. W. Hichens, University of Witswaterstrand Press, Johannesburg, 1940. The family name was dropped in the 1979 publication Muyaka by Mohamed H. Abdulaziz. He identified him as Muyaka bin Haji of Mombasa. Here the place is given prominence in place

of the family name, Al-Ghassaniy. This should signify to the reader the trend and political views of the time.

10. Morton S Freeman, The Story Behind the Word, ISI Press, Philadelphia, 1985.

11. To a Muslim Mswahili the Qur'an forbids the use of defaming and offensive names. Nor defame nor be sarcastic to each other. Nor call each other by offensive nicknames, connoting weakedness ... Sura 49:11. There are several sunnas, i.e., traditions of the Prophet Muhammad, in which he is said to urge his followers to give their children good names and to shun bad ones. One of the hadiths (traditions) states that on the day of judgment human beings will be called by their own names and the names of their fathers and therefore they should keep good names. Muslim scholars also relate the importance of the name to the importance of the word. Africans of other regions use praise-names to bestow a positive image.

12. The Yorubas in Nigeria express the influence of a name on a person in their expression Oruko ni roni "It is name that always has a major influence on someone".

13. The custom of calling a child by his or her day of birth occurs also in parts of West Africa. A Ghanaian boy born on Saturday is called Kwame while the girl is Ameah or Ama; Kwesi or Kwashire is a boy born on Sunday and the girl is Akosua or Awashe. Kwodwo/Kodjo/Kedjo is a boy born on Monday and the girl is Adwoah/Adojoo/Adojoa. Kwabena and Abenah are born on Tuesday (Some dialects have Kobla and Abla). Kwaku and Akuah/Aku on Wednesday, Yaw and Yaa on Thursday but some use Kwao and Awo. Kofi and Afuah are born on Friday.
The same practice was used in some European countries, where, for example, a baby born on a Sunday might be called Dominick, i.e. born on the day of dominus, the Lord.

14. See A.Yusuf Ali, *The Holy Qur'an* , Sura VII v. 180:

The most beautiful names belong to God: So call on Him by them; But shun such men as use profanity in His names; For what they do, they will soon be requited. See also Muhammad Marmaduke Pickthall, *The Glorious Qur'aan* who refers to them as 'the fairest names' p. 165. Besides being used in daily prayers and as personal names, these names are written on talismans and on artifacts for decorative and protective purpose.

15. After certain letters, e.g. r, t, d, s, s, the l of Abdul- is assimilated and takes the pronunciation of that letter. People use other attributes as well as the ninety-nine which constitute the Beautiful Names.

16. Muhammad Taqee Uthmani writes to dissuade parents from shortening their children's names and using nicknames. See his Foreword to Hathurani's *Names For Muslim Children*.

17. On the other hand, many Swahili names start with A, S, B and H. Names beginning with O and E are common in some other African languages and are of frequent occurrence in parts of West Africa.

18. Many discrepancies occur in the pronunciation not simply of people's names, but of the names of places, of course. This, too, may be because of their spellings. For instance, Darsalama not only in writing but in pronunciation has become Dar-es-Salaam, The Sultanate of 'Umaan is pronounced Oman. Al-Qaahira has become Cairo, Al-uqsur is Luxor, Finiiqy is Phoenicia, Al-Hind is India. Except for the natives of these places or linguists, who may know the other names, most people use the Anglicized western version which might be shorter or easier for a non-native to pronounce. Too often, however, they also assume it to be the only form. This view may be hazardous in historical reconstruction and analyses.

19. In the United States and Europe in general, in formal situations, a person is usually addressed by his last name,

e.g. Mr. Jones. The use of a first name in such a situation was once considered a sign of familiarity or disrespect although this is changing now. The Waswahili, on the other hand, have always used the first name in address but preceded by a title of respect, e.g. not simply Ali, but Bwana Ali, not Asha but Bi Asha or Mama Asha.

20. A well known African historian and geographer Abu Muhammad 'Abdallah bin 'Umar Al-wazzan of Fez (d. A.H.1278/1526 A.D.) lost his original name to that of John Leo Africanus when he was captured and converted to Christianity in the fifteenth century. Names of a different kind undergoing change are the many African place names which fell out of use in the colonial era have been reclaimed. Thus the Gold Coast, the Belgian Congo, Northern Rhodesia, Southern Rhodesia and Mozambique are now called Ghana, Zaire, Zimbabwe, Zambia and Msumbiji, respectively. Some African-American scholars are now using Q-M-T-(Kemet) instead of Egypt. Similar changes of names occur in other parts of the world, of course, as we have recently seen in what was the Soviet Union.

21. Sometimes the name of a famous foreign leader or a celebrity is chosen, such as George Washington, Fidel Castro, Mao Tse Tung or King George. The parents may also use a name because they like the way it sounds such as the names Kim, Jeff. or Natasha. An English equivalent of a name is sometimes used because of its closeness to the Swahili or Arabic name as in the case of Janet for Jannat (heaven), Sal for Salim (safe), Sam for Saamii (exalted), Hass for Hassan (good), Sabrina for Sabri (patience) and William, when referring to a woman, for walyma (feast). Occasionally, a name such as Moses is used instead of its Swahili variant Musa, and Mary instead of Maryam.

22. There are many non-Muslim Africans with European or Christian names. Among the leaders of past and present time are Julius Nyerere, Milton Obote, Patrick

Lumumba, Tom Mboya and Hastings Kamuzu Banda. With the independence of African states from colonial rule, and as a way of establishing their identity, some Africans have changed their Christian names to indigenous African names. The famous East African novelists Ngugi wa Thiong'o and the president of Zaire Mobotu Sese Seko are among these. Okot p'Bitek, the eminent Ugandan writer, in his well-known poems - Song of Ocol, Song of Lawino and Song of Prisoner - changed his Christian name Jekeri to Bitek, his grandfather's name, presenting a model for what he was promoting - decolonization and an appreciation of African values.

23. Shaaban bin Robert, *Maisha Yangu na Baada ya Miaka Hamsini*, Thomas Nelson, Dasr-es-Salaam, 1949/1966.

24. Mwana Mwarabu tells us that in this poem she wishes to praise the Lord who is one and eternal and is the ruler of the universe. He is compassionate and kind to the good and the bad. She writes:

He is the master, our master.
He is the ruler, our ruler.
He is the creator of those,
Ignorant and knowledgeable.
He is knowledge.

The poem focuses on the strength and power of a talisman, a wriitten expression of a beleief. The poem may be found in a collection of Swahili poems compiled by Ernst Dammann, *Dichtungen in der Lamu*, Vol. 50-52, *Mundart der Suaheli*, Hamburg, 1940. It has never been translated into English.

25. This may be one of the reasons that women are usually not mentioned in Swahili literary accounts and only a few appear in literary anthologies. Albert S. Gerard in *African Language and Literature:An Introduction to the Literary History of Sub-Saharan Africa*, 1981, notes: The middle years of the nineteenth century saw the appearance of the first Swahili woman writer on record (p.13).

Similar views are conveyed by Arne Zetterstern, the editor of *East African Literature: An Anthology* (1983:viii) who claims: The earliest poem in Swahili preserved in manuscript is the Hamziya, a hymn translated by the poet Aidarus (a man) from an Arabic original in 1652 A.H. (1745 A.D.). Both authors base their erroneous conclusions on Jan Knappert's earlier statement in *Traditional Swahili Poetry*, E.J. Brill,1967 (p.3).

26. Asante, ibid.
27. Ibid., p.26. Asante also lists this name among those identified as being from the Eastern Region.
28. People may use names designated to them, consciously or unconsciously, regardless of their original connotations. An example is the term Negro to refer to the Blacks of Africa, Asia and the Americas. Webster's *New Twentieth Century Dictionary*, 1979 derives 'Negro' from the Latin 'niger' meaning black. According to Basil Hargrave 'negro' was the Spanish name for a black African, derived from the Latin 'niger'. He suggests that the original home of the negro race was probably Africa south of the Sahara, the greater part of Southern India, and a large part of Australasia. Eric Partridge adds that 'The Greek anigros ... impure, unclean, akin to Greek knephas, darkness, and knephaios dark, sombre...'. The word has also been identified as meaning a dead person in Greek! (See Dawud Hakim (Foreword) who cites Shipley). In Arabic the equivalent word is nukur which means unknown, disowned, cast off or alienated. This is not a favorable image, but it depicts a historical change in the usage of the word.
Despite its etymology the name has been used, and by some is still being used, to refer to the black people of the world and it has also labeled the Negritude movement. Such a name is renounced and disdained by some for its condescending negative hidden image. However, Edward W. Blyden, a distinguished nineteenth century black scholar, who travelled widely in Africa uses the

word Negro in the title of his famous work and criticizes the anthropologist Bosworth Smith, for writing it with a small 'n'. This is an excellent example of how terms change their original concepts in time and place.

29. According to Robert Needham Cust in his A Sketch of the Modern languages of Africa: The name Berber is derived from the great Arian term for "Foreigner" which appears in the Sanskrit, Greek, and Latin languages...This ancient name , applied in contempt, lives as the recognized term Barbary... It means speakers of a foreign language, 1883, p.98.

30. Other degrading labels for Africans are Bushman and Pygmy. The former are now lumped together with the Hottentots and identified as the Khoisan. The first part of the name is said to have been derived from the "Hottentot's" word for people Khoikhoi and the second sa is "Bushmens' which means gathering food. The final -n indicates the plural form of the word. Hence the new term Khoisan stand for food gathering people. According to one African linguist, Estavan Fodor, both parts of the word - k'oi and san mean 'men'. The use of the word people to refer to a language group is also seen in the word Bantu coined around 1869 by Bleek to refer to those African languages which are related and are spoken south of the Sahara.

31. Several African historians have suggested that Solomon, Moses, Christ and Mary were first portrayed as Africans and that only later the European renaissance artists and literalists represented them Caucasian with non-African physical features.

32. Ngugi wa Thiong'o uses names to identify characters in his English novel, *Petals of Blood*.

33. An understanding of the meanings of the names of characters in Swahili folk tales and novels conveys better the theme and the events that are narrated in the story. Each name adds some characterization and plays a role in the framework of the whole story. Note the

opposition in Ismail's epic between the two leading characters, the medicine men: Shambi bin Dima, the foul and nasty, and Nguvumali, Power is wealth. One misses much of the characterization when reading the translation The Medicine Man by Peter Leinhardt, .

34. Cited by William Chittick, *Spiritual Teachings of Rumi*, Albany, SUNY, 1983,p. 270.

35. The significance of this identity was acknowledged by the prominent black leader who was first known as Malcolm Little became Malcolm X, and was later honored as El-Hajj Malik-Shabazz.

36. Swahili names also came into American story telling around this time. *Moja Means One* by Muriel Feelings, New York, E.P. Dutton, 1976 is a book of counting with illustrations of East African scenes. Joy Anderson's *Juma and the Magic Jin*, New York, Lothrop, Lee & Shepard Books, 1986 is a story about a little boy in Lamu in Kenya and it contains several Swahili phrases. There are many others. It is hoped that this name book may be of use to writers of such children's books.

37. The choice of the name African-American is an indication that its bearer is a person of African descent who was born in America. It allows him or her to identify with both cultures. It is also a step towards regaining ones lost heritage.

38. The holiday of Kwanza was introduced in California by Dr. Maulana Karenga in 1966. The name was originally spelt Kwanza but in the past three years people have begun to adopt the spelling Kwanzaa. The additional vowel may have been added to give the word seven letters representing the seven days, the seven candles and the seven principles. The terms for the seven principles emanate also from Imamu Amiri Baraka's ideas of Black value system and are Swahili.

39. Abdallah makes this statement in his introduction to Damali's *Golden Names for an African People*.